APPLE WATCH SERIES 7 S

An Insanely Simple Manual for the Non-Tech-Savvy to Master the Latest Apple Watch and WatchOS 8 in No Time

Craig Walton

Table of contents

Introduction

The Apple Watch Series 8 is the latest addition to the Apple Watch family, offering a new high-g accelerometer and improved gyroscope that can detect severe car crashes and automatically alert emergency services. It also features a new temperature sensor that enables advanced cycle tracking features including retrospective ovulation estimates. These features, along with the redesigned features of the Series 7, make the Apple Watch Series 8 an excellent tool for seniors looking to track their health and fitness.

The Apple Watch Series 7 has been redesigned with softer, more rounded edges and a unique refractive edge that allows full-screen watch faces and applications to blend seamlessly with the case's curve. Contour and Modular Duo are two new watch faces designed specifically for Apple's new Series 7 Apple Watch. Apple Pay has also been supported on the Watch, allowing purchases and checkouts to be made online or through a contactless terminal. Because of the smaller bezels, the new versions have a larger, redesigned retina display with more screen real estate. The display's breaking edge almost curls into the shell. There are UI upgrades and two distinct watch faces to take advantage of the larger screens.

The Apple Watch Series 7 includes the same health features as previous generations, including blood oxygen monitoring, electrocardiogram (ECG), sleep monitoring, fall detection, and loud sound detection. In an emergency, it also supports Apple Pay transactions and SOS calls. In the 7 Series, Apple offers GPS and GPS + LTE variants. Even when no iPhone is present, Apple Watch devices with LTE connectivity can be handled over LTE. Midnight, Starlight, Green, Blue, and (PRODUCT) RED are the five new body colors for aluminum vehicles. Stainless steel still has silver, graphite, and gold, while titanium has silver and space black. Apple still sells stainless steel Apple Watch Hermès editions and aluminum Apple Watch Nike variants.

The interface has been improved to take advantage of the larger screens, and two new watch faces have been created. The OLED Always-On Low Power Display (LTPO) technology introduced with the 5 Series is carried over to the 7 Series, allowing users to always see their watch face, time, or recently active app. This comprehensive guide will teach you everything you need to know about the Apple Watch Series 7 and 8. This includes beginner and advanced tips and tricks to assist Apple Watch Series 7 and 8 senior users in mastering and operating the smartwatch like a pro. The manual is aimed at both beginners and seniors, as well as those making the switch from other smartwatches to the Apple Watch Series 7 and 8 for the first time. It has been meticulously organized with pictures and step-by-step instructions to maximize the user's experience and mastery.

Ready? Let's get started!

Chapter 1: Brief History of the Apple Watch Since 2015

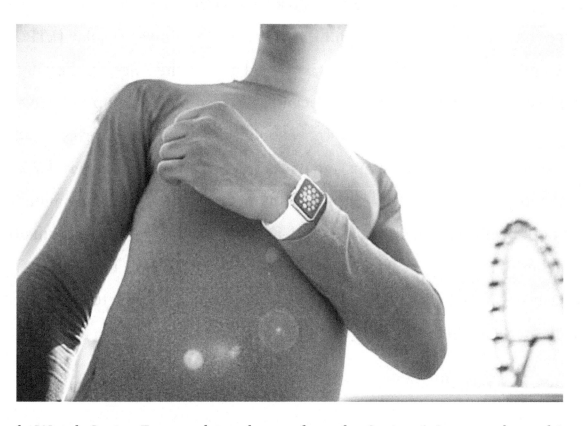

The Apple Watch Series 7 was released to replace the Series 6. It was released in September 2021. The Apple Watch Series 7 is based on previous Apple Watch models but with a more rounded design and a few significant new features, such as larger screens, increased durability, and faster charging.

There's another Apple Watch that looks like a clock. A year after the Series 6 dispatch, we had our first authority look at the replacement. Even though there are some helpful updates, it is known as the Watch Series 7.

They combine an additional complement screen with slimmer sides and the most recent display dimensions. This means there's enough space for a full console, and the IP6X dust resistance complements the current WR50 water resistance. You also get a significantly faster burden and fall recognition while accelerating and an additional shading range. In any case, the Series 7 continues to work with existing Apple Watch bands and groups.

The 2020 Watch Series 6 is replaced by the wearable device, which joins Apple's smartwatch lineup alongside the 2017 Watch SE and Watch Series 3.

On September 14, 2021, the Watch Series 7 was released. We would have expected the delivery date or pre-orders to be confirmed simultaneously, but this was not the case. Apple has announced that the Series 7 will be available later this fall, but no other details have been released.

Series 7 of Watch may be released before the end of 2021. There will most likely be a pre-request window of one to fourteen days before the device is discounted. Apple may reveal more information as events unfold in the coming months.

The Series 7 device, unveiled in September 2021, is the most recent version of the Apple Watch, which was introduced in 2015 and replaced with the Series 6. With a more rounded design, the Series 7 device improves on previous Apple Watch models and introduces significant new features such as larger screens, superior durability, and rapid charging.

Apple watches have long been popular as smartwatches, and the Series 7 is no exception. This device is not significantly different from the previous model (Series 6), but this is not necessarily a disadvantage. The Series 7 improves on Apple's Series 6's refined software experience, sleek design, and useful fitness features.

It has a larger display with a QWERTY keyboard, new color options, quick charging, and increased durability for the first time, with no price difference from its predecessor. Of course, it's not perfect; the battery life could be better, and the sleep tracking feature lags behind the competition. It is, however, unquestionably the best smartwatch for iPhone users, which is why it is ranked first.

While the larger screen is the most noticeable change in Series 7, several other notable changes exist. The design is long-lasting and dust-resistant for the first time; it charges up to 33% faster than the Series 6, and the aluminum casing now comes in various innovative color options.

Aside from that, it has all of the features of the Series 6 and more premium features not found on the Apple Watch SE, such as an always-on display and the ability to take ECG readings from the wrist.

The Series 7 is a refined version of the Series 6 rather than a significant upgrade. The Series 7 is an appealing option for first-time Apple Watch buyers and those upgrading from a previous model, as it costs the same as the Series 6.

There's no reason to spend $400 on this device if you already own a Series 5 or 6. This device will feel like a significant upgrade if you have an older model, such as a Series 2 or 3.

A New Look and Improved User Interface

Since its debut in 2015, Apple hasn't done much to update the watch, but the current iteration has a new layout and features that set it apart from its predecessors.

Apple replaced the previous 40 and 44 mm watch sizes with new 41 and 45 mm sizes, larger displays, and improved screen technology.

The Apple Watch Series 7 "combines all of the excellent features of the Apple Watch with our largest and most sophisticated display yet," according to Apple COO Jeff Williams.

The 45 mm model will have a 396 x 484-pixel resolution, and Williams claims that the new retina display offers more than 20% more screen space than the Series 6 and more than 50% more screen space than the Series 5.

"It's a brilliant design that maximizes the screen surface while slightly changing the overall proportions of the watch. Furthermore, the shape of the watch has been improved. The casing and display of the Series 7 have softer, rounded corners. The new display refracts light at its edges to create a delicate wraparound effect that blends in with the case's curve," Williams said. "When you take your wrist off, it's up to 70% brighter inside, making it even easier to see the time quietly; we completely optimized this new display's user interface, which is an industry first."

The buttons on the Apple Watch have been updated and enlarged to match the size and shape of the watch, according to Lauren Braun, Apple Watch product manager.

According to Braun, there are also new ways to input text, such as a full keyboard that you can tap or slide from letter to letter. The watch also uses machine learning to predict the words you type.

Chapter 2: Different Models, Prices, and Specs in A Table

Features of Apple Watch Series 7

Design

The Apple Watch Series 7 has the same rounded and square shape as the previous generation, but it now comes in two casing sizes to accommodate your preference and wrist size: 41 mm and 45 mm.

The black ceramic and crystal back of all Apple Watch Series 7 models houses four LED clusters and four photodiodes for heart monitoring features such as blood oxygen monitoring, heart rate, and ECG.

The Apple Watch has a Digital Crown for scrolling and navigating and a Side Button for bringing up frequently used apps, accessing emergency services, and confirming Apple Pay purchases, among other things.

The Apple Watch is available in three materials: titanium, stainless steel, and aluminum. The weight of each Series 7 model is shown below:

41 mm	45 mm
32.0g aluminum	38.8g aluminum
42.3 Stainless steel	51.5g stainless steel
37.0g Titanium	45.1g Titanium

Durability

The IP6X dust-resistant rating of the Apple Watch Series 7 makes it more durable in environments such as deserts or the beach.

The watch retains WR50 water resistance, indicating that it can be submerged in deep water due to glue and seals. Because of its 50-meter diving rating, the Apple Watch can be used while swimming in the ocean or pool. The Apple Watch is designed for shallow water, not scuba diving or other high-velocity water activities.

Display

The Apple Watch Series 7 has a larger screen that is nearly 20% larger.

When the wrist is lowered, the screen blacks out to save battery life, but critical features such as the watch hands remain illuminated. The screen will be fully illuminated if you touch the watch's face or raise your hand.

Storage

The Apple Watch Series 7 has 32 GB of storage for podcasts, music, apps, and more.

Cost

The Watch Series 7 starts at £379/$399, roughly the same as the Watch Series 6. Apple Watch prices have been fairly consistent in recent years, with a slight decrease in the UK market last year. At the time of market dispatch, the three archetype models were evaluated.

In Apple's wearable product line, the Watch Series 7 has replaced the Watch Series 6, which the company will no longer sell:

- Apple Watch Series 3 starts at £199/$199.

- Apple Watch Series SE: Prices begin at £ 269/$ 279.

- Apple Watch Series 6: starting at € 379/€ 399

New Strategy

The Watch Series 7 design has been refreshed by Apple, which is the most significant surface level change in years. The most noticeable difference is that the Watch Series 7's presentation now extends nearly to the edge of the dial.

This is made possible by reducing the bezels significantly. At 1.7 mm thick, they are 40% thinner than the Watch 6. This gives the Watch 7 a more modern appearance while not significantly altering the device's overall size. To be honest, the new watch works perfectly with Watch 6 wristbands and groups.

New Screen Dimensions

It's a minor change but could significantly impact the device's usability.

According to Apple, the Series 7 has nearly 20% more screen space than its predecessor. It also implies no room for a standard console that uses swiping signals and standard composing. When sending an instant message or email, it's a useful alternative to the current composing and voice input options.

The always visible has also been updated. The inside is now 70% brighter, allowing you to check the time or notice something quickly.

Charge Faster

The battery life on the Watch Series 7 was supposed to be improved, but this has not happened. Apple claims that a single charge will provide 18 hours of normal usage.

One area that has been updated is stacking speed. Another USB-C appealing cushion allows for 33% faster speeds than the Watch Series 6. As demonstrated, it can charge from 0% to 90% in less than an hour.

New Wellness Features

The new wellness features of the Watch Series 7 are aimed at anyone who rides a bicycle regularly. Cycling is one of the modes that can now be activated naturally, much like a programmed interruption and resume capabilities.

Apple Watch OS 8

Regardless of how long it takes for the Watch Series 7 to arrive, the most recent version of watchOS 8 will be installed.

Apple's most recent software update announced at WWDC in June 2021 will concentrate on Photographs and News, well-being, Rest, Staying Fit, and Care, as well as improved support for brilliant home units and some new Apple Wallet highlights.

There's also Assistive Touch, which lets you control the clock with motions and set up Siri accounts on the device.

The Apple Watch will get the iPhone's representation photograph mode, allowing you to see dramatically improved photos of your loved ones. It also allows for renaming the Inhale application to Care, which now includes a respite mode for unwinding with relaxing activities and a rundown of Careful Minutes.

The Apple Watch and Climate Change

The Apple Watch Series 7 contains far more reusable material than any previous Apple Watch, including rare earth elements that have been 100 percent reused in all magnets. In keeping with Apple's environmental commitment, the Taptic Motor has approximately 100% reused tungsten throughout the item and 100 percent encased aluminum models. The Apple Watch Series 7 is also free of potentially harmful synthetic compounds such as mercury, PVC, beryllium, and BFR.

Apple's global business activities are carbon neutral, and the company plans to have net environmental impacts across the organization by 2030, including manufacturing supply chains and all product life cycles. All Apple products are carbon neutral, from component manufacturing to collection, transportation, client use, and stacking to reusing and material recovery.

Battery Life of the Apple Watch 7

The Apple Watch 7 has the same 18-hour battery life as the previous Series 6 and Series 5 Apple Watches. We would have preferred to see progress in this area, but we must believe that improved presentation and show quality will justify the daily workload.

On the other hand, the new USB-C connection allows the Apple Watch 7 to be fully charged up to 33% faster. If you don't mind, this new charging link will also help other Apple Watch models charge faster. It is not a distinguishing feature of the Apple Watch 7.

Processor and Accessibility

Apple regularly updates Apple Watch processors, and the Series 7 will be no exception. The Watch Series 7 is said to have a more modest S7 chip that scales down the module using two-sided innovation.

The smaller S7 microprocessor, on the other hand, will make more room for these extra components, with the extra space being used for a larger battery or healthy lifestyle detectors. Apple is also expected to show off progress on remote accessibility and a refined U1 super broadband chip.

New Watch Faces and Programming

The Apple Watch Series 7 will include a selection of watch faces optimized for the largest screens.

A measured Max dial provides advanced time and a minor annoyance like temperature, while the larger extra complications are stacked on top of each other at the base. It is similar to Infographics Secluded but can have multiple significant ambiguities.

The time and current time stream show how a Continuum responds to changes.

Another world-time face allows customers to view all 24 time zones simultaneously. The time zones are displayed on the external dial, while the time in each area is displayed on the internal dial.

Another Hermes watch face has hourly changing numbers, and a Nike watch face has numbers that vary based on a person's development.

Apple intends to introduce new Time with Run and Audio Meditations capabilities with the release of the Apple Watch Series 7, which will complement the Time to Walk option introduced earlier this year.

Difference Between Apple Watch Series 7 And Others

iPhone Life MAGAZINE	Apple Watch			Fitbit						
	Series 7	Series SE	Series 3	Sense	Versa 3	Versa 2	Charge 5	Luxe	Inspire 2	Ace 3
Cost	$399+	$279+	$199+	$299.95	$229.95	$179.95	$179.95	$149.95	$99.95	$79.95
Compatibility	iOS Only	iOS Only	iOS Only	iOS, Android	iOS, Android	iOS, Android	iOS, Android	iOS, Android	iOS, Android	iOS, Android
Battery Life	Up to 18 Hours	Up to 18 Hours	Up to 18 Hours	Up to 6 Days	Up to 6 Days	Up to 6 Days	Up to 7 Days	Up to 5 Days	Up to 10 Days	Up to 8 Days
Built-In GPS	√	√	√	√	√	-	-	-	-	-
Sleep, Step, & Exercise Minute Tracking	√	√	√	√	√	√	√	√	√	√
Skin Temperature	-	-	-	√	√	√	√	√	√	√
Tracking	√	√	√	-	-	-	-	-	-	-
LTE Compatibility	√	√	√	-	-	-	-	-	-	-
Multiple Size Options	√	√	√	√	√	√	√	√	√	√
Water Resistant & Pool Safe	√	√	√	√	√	√	√	√	√	√
EDA (Mental Health) Sensor	-	-	-	√	-	-	√	-	-	-

	Apple Watch Series 5	Apple Watch Series 4	Apple Watch Series 3
Sizes	40 mm or 44 mm	40 mm or 44 mm	38 mm or 42 mm
Display	759 sq mm / 977 sq mm	759 sq mm / 977 sq mm	563 sq mm / 740 sq mm
Always-On	Yes	No	No
Processor	Dual-core S5 + W3 wireless chip	Dual-core S4 + W3 wireless chip	Dual-core S3 + W2 wireless chip
Finishes	Aluminum/stainless steel/ titanium/ceramic	Aluminum/stainless steel	Aluminum
Storage	32GB	16GB	8GB/16GB (cellular)
Features	Compass, ECG, 2nd gen. heart rate monitor, 50% louder speaker, GymKit, Haptic Digital Crown	ECG, 2nd gen. heart rate monitor, 50% louder speaker, GymKit, Haptic Digital Crown	Heart rate monitor, GymKit
Connectivity	Wi-Fi, Bluetooth 5.0	Wi-Fi, Bluetooth 5.0	Wi-Fi, Bluetooth 4.0
Battery life	Up to 18 hours	Up to 18 hours	Up to 18 hours
Dimensions	44 x 38 x 10.7 mm 40 x 34 x 10.7 mm	44 x 38 x 10.7 mm 40 x 34 x 10.7 mm	38.6 x 33.3 x 11.4 mm 42.5 x 36.4 x 11.4 mm
Price (MSRP)	From $399	Discontinued	From $199

	Apple Watch Series 6	Apple Watch SE	Apple Watch Series 5
Size	40, 44 mm	40, 44 mm	40, 44 mm
Display	Always on Retina	Retina	Always on LTPO
Processor	S6	S5	S5
Sensor	Blood Oxygen, ECG, GPS, Compass, Barometric, Altimeter, Accelerometer, Gyro, Ambient light	Heart Sensor, GPS, Compass, Barometric, Altimeter, Accelerometer, Gyro, Ambient light	Heart Sensor with ECG, GPS, Compass, Barometric, Altimeter, Accelerometer, Gyro, Ambient light

Chapter 3: Basic Terminology About the Main Functions of Buttons

- **The Digital Crown Buttons:** The Digital Crown is the dial or rotating mechanism on the Home button. It performs different functions depending on the app in which you use it.

- **The Home Button:** The Home button on the Digital Crown can be found on your Apple Watch display's left or right side. You can alter your Apple Watch's orientation and the position of the buttons.

- **Side Button:** The Side button on your Apple Watch is the longer, thinner button next to the Digital Crown. Depending on the orientation of your watch, it may be above or below the Digital Crown.

- **Instantaneous Editing**: To fix text issues, use the Digital Crown to scroll precisely to the area that needs to be edited.

- **Keyboard Layout:** QuickPath and QWERTY keyboard layouts (U.S. English and Simplified Chinese only, Apple Watch Series 7 only). To enter text, use the full QWERTY keyboard. Simply tap each character individually or use QuickPath to swipe between letters without lifting your finger.

- **Mindfulness App:** The Mindfulness app's new Reflect function assists you in developing a meditation practice by focusing on a brief, thought-provoking subject. You can listen to guided meditations directly on your Apple Watch if you have an Apple Fitness+ membership.

- **Workout:** Experiment with new workouts. The new Pilates routine will help you strengthen your core, whereas Tai Chi will help you clear your mind and relax.

- **Focus:** By allowing only the alerts you choose, Focus helps you stay present at the moment when concentration is required. Select one of the pre-suggested Focuses, such as working or working out, or sync a custom Focus created on your iPhone, iPad, or Mac.

- **Add Contact:** Use the new Contacts app on your Apple Watch to explore, add, or modify contacts quickly. Start several timers in the Timers app while using Siri to identify each one.

- **Multiple Timers**: Timing is essential when preparing a multicourse meal. Begin in the Timers app several times as you begin to use Siri to identify each.

● **Volume**: Control Center displays real-time headphone audio levels when you listen to media on watchOS 8.

Chapter 4: How to Set Up the Apple Watch for the First Time and Pair it with iPhone

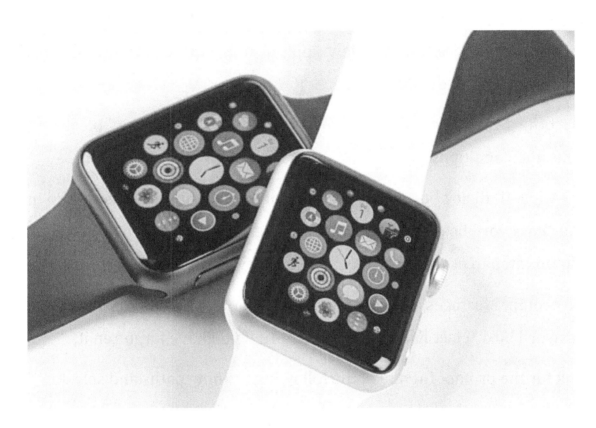

Set Up Your Apple Watch

Bring the iPhone close to the Apple Watch, then press the iPhone's Continue button. It is important to note that eSIM comes pre-installed and cannot be removed. Check that you have completed the online activation process before configuring your device. For more information, activate your phone, SIM card, or other devices.

To personalize the device, select Configure for me. Select Assign to Family Member to assign to a family member. Family members who do not own an iPhone can take advantage of Apple Watch features and benefits with WatchOS 7 or Family Setup.

1. To pair the Apple Watch, place it on the iPhone and align it with the viewfinder below. Select Manual pairing to connect the clock manually.

2. Choose Restore from Backup and follow the on-screen instructions to copy your content, or choose Set Up as a New Apple Watch to proceed without transferring data from your old device.

3. Select the desired wrist (left or right). Before clicking "I Agree," please read the terms and conditions.

4. The Apple ID dialog box will appear. Sign in by entering your password in the Enter Password box. Select Forgot your password if you have forgotten it. Click Skip this step to proceed without associating your Apple ID.

5. The prompt Messages will appear. Sign in by entering your password in the Enter Password box. Select Forgot your password if you have forgotten it.

6. Look for the prompt for one of the following training paths and select it. View the Siri prompt and then choose the appropriate option.

7. After checking the Shared Settings message, click OK.

8. Display the prompt for bold text and font size. After adjusting the text settings, select the desired option.

9. To create an Apple Watch password, select Create Password and follow the on-screen instructions. If you want to create a password longer than four digits, click

Add a long password and follow the on-screen instructions. Select Do not add a password to disable the passcode.

10.   Choose one of the options under Keep the Apple Watch Prompt Updated. After reading the emergency message, press the Continue button.

11.   To get started with mobile phone service, click Set up cellular. To proceed without configuring a mobile service, select No now. Install All to install all of the available applications. Select "Select" later to install applications later.

12.   Display the application view prompt, then select the appropriate application view.

The Apple Watch and iPhone are now in sync. When you're finished, click OK. The Apple Watch is now available for purchase and use.

Pairing with Your iPhone

The setup assistants on the iPhone and Apple Watch collaborate to help you pair and configure your Apple Watch.

After the Apple Watch has been properly initialized, press the language button to select your preferred language and follow the on-screen instructions. When prompted, move the iPhone so that the Apple Watch is visible in the iPhone's camera viewfinder when taking photos. This creates a link between the two devices.

The screen displays a pairing visual, with a left arm holding an Apple Watch and a right hand holding the appropriate iPhone in the foreground. To connect to the Apple Watch, use the iPhone's connection instructions and the coupling example, with the Apple Watch visible in the iPhone's viewfinder.

After connecting, finish the setup by following the instructions on the iPhone and Apple Watch screens. If you're having trouble pairing the camera, select Pair Apple Watch. Manually follow the on-screen instructions at the bottom of the iPhone screen.

Wrap your Apple Watch around your wrist, then press and hold the side button to turn it on. Hold your iPhone near the watch and follow the onscreen instructions. To prepare an Apple Watch for a family member, tap Set up for a family member.

How to Disconnect an Apple Watch

1. Activate the Apple Watch app on your iPhone.
2. Touch My Watch at the top of the screen, then All Watches.
3. Click the About button next to the Apple Watch you want to unpair, then tap Unpair Apple Watch.

Pairing Multiple Apple Watches

You can connect a second Apple Watch like you linked the first. Wait for your iPhone to display the Apple Watch connection screen before pressing Pair.

Alternatively, follow these steps:

1. Activate the Apple Watch app on your iPhone.

2. Click My Watch at the top of the screen, then All Watches.

3. Follow the onscreen instructions after tapping Add a watch.

How to Quickly Switch to Another Apple Watch

Your iPhone will recognize the paired Apple Watch you are wearing and automatically connect to it. Raise your wrist and put on another Apple Watch. You may also choose an Apple Watch manually:

1. On your iPhone, activate the Apple Watch app.

2. At the top of the screen, click My Watch, and then tap All Watches.

3. Disable automatic switching.

How to Connect an Apple Watch to a Brand-New iPhone

If you wish to sync your Apple Watch with your new iPhone after it was previously associated with your old iPhone, follow these steps:

1. Use iCloud Backup to back up your iPhone with your Apple Watch.

2. Set up your new iPhone. On the Apps & Data screen, choose to restore from an iCloud backup and choose the latest backup.

3. Continue the iPhone set up and, when prompted, select your Apple Watch with your new iPhone.

4. When the iPhone setup is complete, your Apple Watch will ask you to pair it with the new iPhone. Tap OK on your Apple Watch and enter the passcode.

Chapter 5: Basic Settings

How to Activate Your Watch

Follow these steps to get your Apple Watch up and running:

- **When the Apple Watch shows a blank display:** If the Apple Watch initially appears blank, hold the side button until you see the Apple logo (you may see a blank screen at first), then wait for the watch face to appear.
- **To turn it off:** Your Apple Watch should be turned on all the time, but if you need to turn it off, press and hold the side button until the slider display appears, then move the Power Off slider to the right until the watch is turned off.

- **If your Apple Watch has been idle for an extended period, it is recommended to restart it:** Simply extend your wrist. When you remove the Apple Watch from your wrist, it goes back to sleep mode. Touching the display or pressing the Digital Crown on the device's side will also activate Apple Watch. The home screen of the Apple Watch, from which you can launch apps by tapping them. To get to the home screen, press and hold the Digital Crown for a few seconds on the watch face.

- **When the Apple Watch wakes up, you can choose whether to display the watch face or return to your previous position:** To enable the feature, go to the home screen's Settings icon, then General > Wake Screen, and turn on Wake Screen on Wrist Raise.

- **You can also use the Apple Watch app on your iPhone:** Select My Watch from the dropdown menu, then General. Wrist detection should be enabled by default; therefore, double-check this setting before tapping Wake Screen. The Apple Watch's General Settings screen appears, with the pointer pointing to the option "Activate on Wrist Raise." To configure it, press and hold the button.

- **Enter your security code in the following format:** If you take your Apple Watch off your wrist or wear it too loosely, the next time it wakes up, it will prompt you for your passcode. If you don't have a passcode, the device will prompt you for one. Simply enter your passcode into the number pad that appears.

- **Automatic security:** When you enable wrist detection, your watch will automatically lock when you are not wearing it, saving you time. Open the Apple Watch app on your iPhone and go to My Watch, then General. Allow Wrist

Detection to be turned on. It is impossible to turn off Wrist Detection without also turning off Apple Pay.

- **Manually lock:** Hold the side button until the slider appears, then move the Lock Device slider to the right until it disappears. You will be prompted to enter your passcode again when you first try to use Apple Watch. A Cancel button is located in the upper left-hand corner of the slider screen, along with three sliders labeled Power off, Power Reserve, and Lock Device, and a Cancel button in the top right-hand corner.

- **The Apple Watch should be wiped clean after ten unsuccessful unlock attempts:** You can set Apple Watch to erase its data after ten unsuccessful attempts to unlock it with an incorrect password to protect the contents of your watch if it is lost or stolen. Using your iPhone, launch the Apple Watch app, select My Watch from the dropdown menu, enter your password, and then toggle the Erase Data switch to the On position.

Choose Language or Region

Tap to change the language.

1. Launch the Watch application on your iPhone

2. Click on My Watch, go to General> Language and region, click Custom, and Watch Language.

How to Set Up Apple ID

If prompted, enter your Apple ID password in the box. If you are not prompted, you can sign in later via the Apple Watch app:

1. Sign in first, then navigate to General > Apple ID. Several services that require a cellular phone number will not work on Apple Watch cellular versions unless you connect to iCloud.

2. If Find My isn't enabled on your iPhone, you'll be prompted to enable Activation Lock. If you see the Activation Lock screen, your Apple Watch is already linked to an Apple ID.

3. Enter the Apple ID's email address and password to complete the setup. If you have a previously owned Apple Watch, you may need to contact the previous owner to remove the Activation Lock.

How to Select a Wi-Fi Network

Long-press the bottom of the screen and then slide up to open Control Center. Hold down the Wi-Fi Button, then tap the name of a nearby Wi-Fi network. 802.11b/g/n 2.4GHz Wi-Fi networks are compatible with the Apple Watch.

If your connection requires a password, follow these steps:

1. Enter the password using the Apple Watch's QWERTY keyboard (Apple Watch Series 7 only).

2. Scribble the password characters on the screen with your finger. Using the Digital Crown, select upper- or lower-case letters.

3. Select a password from the list by tapping the Password button.

4. Enter the password using your iPhone's keyboard.

5. Tap the Join button.

Adjust Brightness

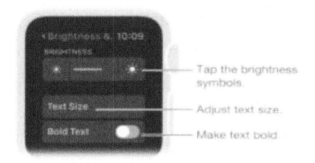

Begin by selecting the Settings button on your phone's home screen, then scroll down to Brightness and Text Size. Depending on your preference, you can adjust the brightness by tapping or cranking on the Digital Crown. Alternatively, open the Apple Watch app on your iPhone and go to My Watch > Brightness & Text Size. To change the brightness of the screen, use the Brightness slider.

Adjust the Volume

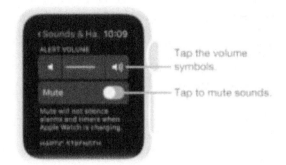

Adjust the level by selecting the Settings icon and scrolling down to the Sounds & Haptics section of the menu. Tap once on the volume buttons or slider to adjust the Alert Volume, then turn the Digital Crown to the desired volume level. Launch the Apple Watch app on an iPhone, go to My Watch, select Sounds & Haptics, and then adjust the Alert Volume slider to the desired level. You can adjust the volume of ringers and alarms by turning the Digital Crown or tapping the volume icons. To turn off Apple Watch, press the Mute button.

Change the Notification Settings for your Watch

By default, the Apple Watch's notification settings are identical to those on the iPhone, although some programs allow you to change how they display notifications.

You can customize how applications notify you. Launch the Watch application. Then click My Watch, followed by Notifications. Choose an application (for example, messages), then an order, and finally a selection, which may contain the following:

- **Allow notification**: Notifications are displayed in the notification center of the application. Notifications are routed straight to the notification center, skipping the Watch entirely and resulting in an audio or visual notification.

- **Notifications Are Disabled**: Notifications are disabled for this program.

Instructions to Set Up Apple Pay on Apple Watch

If you own an Apple Watch and an iPhone, you may be surprised to learn that the two devices work independently regarding Apple Pay.

Regardless of the two devices' usefulness, they use separate, unconnected Passbook applications, which means you can use two different cards. It also implies that you can pay for things without using your iPhone, which is useful if you go for a run or go to the store to get some milk.

The Wallet and Apple Pay software must be launched from the Apple Watch apps for iPhone. A credit or debit card could be linked to a user's account. You can install it on your iPhone by using the Wallet app. If you haven't already, you will be prompted to set a password on your Apple Watch.

Potential hoodlums cannot make installment payments with your smartwatch unless Apple Pay is enabled. When everything is in place, the cycle is very straightforward. It will examine your card with your phone's camera and update any missing data. Following completion, you will receive an email or SMS with a confirmation code that must be entered into the phone application. When checked, the Apple Watch will confirm that you are ready.

Use Spotify on Apple Watch

To utilize Spotify Associate with control your Apple Watch music on all gadgets:

1. Ensure you have downloaded the most recent rendition of the Spotify application on your telephone, PC, or tablet.

2. Utilize the Spotify application to add viable Spotify Interface gadgets.

3. Ensure the two gadgets are associated with a similar Wi-Fi association with a guarantee you can empower this control from your Apple Watch.

Download Music from Spotify to Apple Watch

It's a feature that Spotify customers have requested, and Spotify has finally delivered. You can now download content from Spotify and save it to your Apple Watch to listen to it without being connected to your phone or using LTE.

Before we get into the best method, ensure you have an Apple Watch Series 3 or higher running WatchOS 6 or higher, an LTE or Wi-Fi connection, and a Spotify Premium membership.

How to Fast Charge

The new Apple Watch Series 7 has a fast-charging USB-C cable that can charge your watch quickly.

Is it possible to quickly charge an Apple Watch? Yes! But only if you have an Apple Watch Series 7 and a USB-C quick charging cable. The Series 7 is a powerful device with a slew of cool features, including fast charging. Quick charging allows the Apple Watch to charge up to 80% in 45 minutes. This means you can get enough power to track your sleep in as little as eight minutes!

How to Change your Passcode

1. Open the Settings app on your Apple Watch.

2. Scroll down to Passcode with your finger or the Digital Crown.

3. By clicking Passcode, you can change your password.

4. Enter the passcode that is currently in use.

5. Make a new password for yourself.

Find Your iPhone

1. If your iPhone is nearby, your Apple Watch can assist you in locating it.

2. Tap and hold the bottom of the screen to open Control Center, then tap the Ping iPhone button.

3. Your iPhone emits a tone to help you locate it.

Locate Your Apple Watch

1. If you've misplaced your watch, use Find My to track it.

2. On your iPhone, launch the Find My app.

3. Select your watch from the list by tapping Devices.

4. You can use your watch to play a sound, tap Directions to see directions in Maps, mark it as lost, or delete it.

Turn a Focus On or Off

1. To open Control Center, tap and hold the bottom of the screen, then swipe up.

2. Touch and hold the current Focus button for a few seconds, then tap a Focus.

3. Control Center displays the Do Not Disturb button when no focus is selected.

4. Select an option for Focus: On, On for 1 hour, On until tomorrow morning, or On until I leave.

5. Simply tap the Focus button in Control Center to turn it off.

6. When a Focus is active, its icon appears at the top of the watch face, in apps next to the time, and Control Center.

How to Move or Transfer an Existing Mobile Plan to a Refurbished Apple Watch

Follow these steps to transfer your existing cellular plan from your cellular Apple Watch to another cellular Apple Watch:

1. While wearing your Apple Watch, open the Apple Watch app on your iPhone.

2. Navigate to My Watch, Cellular, and tap the information icon next to your cellular plan.

3. Confirm your selection by tapping Remove [carrier name] plan.

4. You may need to contact your wireless service provider to remove this Apple Watch from your wireless service plan.

5. Remove the old watch, then put on the other mobile Apple Watch, tap My Watch, and finally tap Mobile.

6. To activate your watch for your phone, follow the instructions.

Change or Deactivate Your Next Wake-Up Alarm

The Apple Watch Sleep app displays the evening's sleep schedule. The bedtime is at the top, and the wake-up time is below.

1. On your Apple Watch, launch the Sleep app.

2. Select your current bedtime.

3. To change the wake-up time, tap it, turn the Digital Crown to set a new time, and then tap the Check button.

4. Turn off the Alarm if you don't want your Apple Watch to wake you up in the morning.

5. The changes are only effective for your next wake-up alarm, after which your regular schedule will resume.

6. You can also disable the next wake-up alarm in the Alarms app. Simply tap the alarm in the Sleep | Wake up section, then tap Skip for Tonight.

Make a Phone Call

1. On your Apple Watch, launch the Phone app.

2. Tap Contacts, then use the Digital Crown to scroll.

3. Tap the phone button, then select the person you want to call.

4. Tap FaceTime Audio or a phone number to start a FaceTime audio call.

5. Use the Digital Crown to adjust the volume during the call.

6. Go to Recents and tap a contact to call someone you've recently spoken with. Tap Favorites, then tap a contact to call someone you've marked as a favorite in your iPhone's Phone app.

How to View and Manage Subscriptions

1. On the Apple Watch, look for the Settings app.

2. [Your Username] should be touched.

3. Touch Subscriptions, and then select a subscription to view details such as price and duration.

4. To cancel the subscription, tap Cancel. Some subscriptions on your iPhone will be canceled.

How to Run Shortcuts

1. On Apple Watch, look for the Shortcuts app.

2. Tap the Shortcut.

3. Scroll down to Shortcuts and then choose a Shortcut

How to Include a Complication for the Quick Fix

1. Touch and hold the time dial, then press the Edit button.

2. Swipe to the left to access the Complications screen, then tap Complication.

How to Add Apple Watch to Your Mobile Plan

1. To activate the service later, follow these steps:

2. Look for the Apple Watch app on your iPhone.

3. Tap my watch, and then tap Cellular.

Set a Photo as Your Watch Face

1. Navigate to the Watch app on your iPhone.

2. Select "Face Gallery."

3. Look down and touch "Photos."

4. At this point, you can create an album of your favorite photos.

5. You can select up to 24 photos from your Camera Roll.

Control Your Apple TV with Your Watch

1. Push on the Digital Crown to get to your App List or App Grid, according to your App View.

2. Look for the "Remote" application, which is named Remote and has a blue symbol with a triangle in the middle.

3. Click on a remote.

4. Stand by a second as the watch synchronizes to the Apple TV sets in your home.

5. Pick the Apple TV you need to control.

Get Help in an Emergency

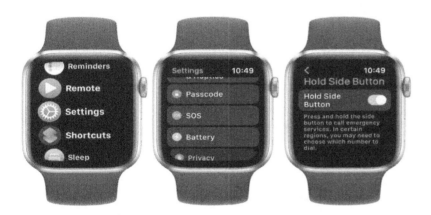

1. Open up the Settings application on the Apple Watch.

2. Look down to "SOS."

3. Empower "Hold Side Button."

4. With the SOS highlight switch on your Apple Watch will start dialing crisis administrations in the nation where you're found, assuming that you hold down the side button.

5. The side button is the adjusted rectangular button beneath the Digital Crown.

Removing Apps from Your Apple Watch

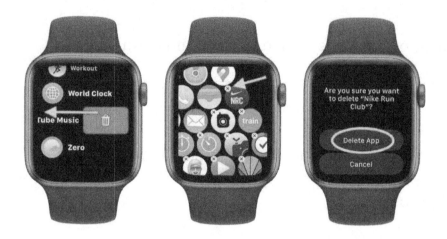

1. Navigate to the Apple Watch's Application View.

2. Long press the screen of the Apple Watch.

3. Choose "Alter Applications."

4. Look through the lattice for applications that you don't need.

5. Click the small "x" on an application's icon to delete it. Confirm that you wanted the application removed.

Sharing a Photo from Your Watch

1. Open the Photos application on the Apple Watch.

2. Select the photo or pictures you need to share and click on them.

3. Click on the little offer symbol on the base right of the photo.

4. Apple watches share photos open. Then, at that point, you can look down and send it to anybody utilizing Messages or Mail.

5. Pick a contact, and a while later, make a message to add one

How to Organize Schooltime

1. To manage the watch, launch the Apple Watch app on your iPhone.

2. Tap All Clocks, then the Family Clocks clock.

3. After you've decided on a time for school, click the Edit Schedule button.

4. Select the days and times for Schooltime to appear on your watch. If you want to create multiple schedules for a single day, start at 8:00 a.m. and tap Add Time until noon, then until 1 p.m. at 15:00.

For example, family members can sign out of Schooltime briefly to check their activity rings. Exit by tapping the screen, rotating the Digital Crown, and pressing the Exit button. If you leave Schooltime within the time limit, the Schooltime clock face will reappear when you lower your wrist if you left Schooltime within the time limit. During non-scheduled hours, schooltime is deactivated until the next scheduled start time or until the Schooltime button in the Control Center is pressed.

Make Apple Watch Text Larger

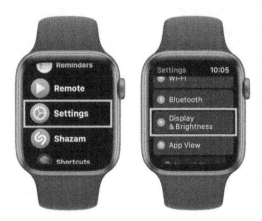

1. Open up the Settings application on Apple Watch.

2. Swipe down to "Show and Brightness" and click it.

3. Click on "Text Size."

4. Tap on the "Aa" on the right half of the presentation to make the message greater. You can also click on the "Aa" symbol on the left side to make it more modest once more.

Enable Airplane Mode

Certain airlines permit you to travel in airplane mode with your Apple Watch (and iPhone). For Watch models with cellular capabilities, airplane mode disables cellular and Wi-Fi but leaves Bluetooth enabled. When you enable airplane mode, you can choose which settings are enabled and which are disabled.

Enable airplane mode on your Apple Watch: To launch Control Center, touch and hold the bottom of the screen, then slide up. Now tap ✈ Inquire with Siri. For example, enable airplane mode.

To enable airplane mode on your Apple Watch and iPhone, follow these steps: open the Apple Watch app on your iPhone, tap My Watch, then General > Airplane Mode, and finally Mirror iPhone. If one device enters airplane mode while your Apple Watch and iPhone are within regular Bluetooth range - approximately 33 feet or ten meters - the other will follow suit.

Change the parameters enabled or disabled in airplane mode: Open the Settings app on your Apple Watch, go to Aircraft Mode, and choose whether Wi-Fi or Bluetooth should be enabled by default while in airplane mode.

Open the Settings app while your Apple Watch is in airplane mode and choose Wi-Fi or Bluetooth. Wi-Fi or Bluetooth appear at the top of the screen when airplane mode is enabled. Even if Mirror iPhone is enabled, you must disable airplane mode on your iPhone and Apple Watch.

Utilize the Watch's Flashlight

To activate the flashlight, press and hold the bottom of the screen, then slide up to launch Control Center. Now tap 🔦 Toggle between modes—steady white light, flashing white light, or steady red light—swipe left.

To turn off the flashlight, swipe down from the watch face's top or press the side button or the Digital Crown.

Switch to Silent Mode

To launch Control Center, touch and hold the bottom of the screen, then slide up. Now tap 🔔 While your Apple Watch is charging, alarms and timers continue to ring in quiet mode.

You may also switch on the quiet mode by opening the Apple Watch app on your iPhone, tapping My Watch, tap Sounds & Haptics, and then tapping Silent Mode.

Tip: When you receive a notification, you can immediately silence your Watch by resting your palm on display for at least three seconds. A touch will confirm that the mute switch is turned on. Cover to Mute should be enabled on your Apple Watch—open the Settings app, select Sounds & Haptics, and then toggle Cover to Mute on.

Activate or Deactivate Walkie Talkie

1. Enter the Walkie-Talkie program.

2. Turn on or off the Walkie-Talkie. If someone wishes to contact you while you are unavailable, a message will appear asking if you wish to speak.

3. Walkie-Talkie can also be activated or deactivated by touching the Walkie-Talkie button in the Control Center.

4. If you enable Silent Mode in the Control Center, you will only be able to hear chimes and your friend's voice.

5. If you can't find the Walkie-Talkie application, reinstall it on your iPhone. FaceTime is required for Walkie-Talkie to function, so if you uninstalled it, reinstall it.

6. Make sure FaceTime is turned on. Enter the settings application, select FaceTime, and turn it on.

7. Start the FaceTime program. Make a call to ensure that you have correctly configured the FaceTime application.

8. Start your Watch again.

9. Reboot your phone.

How to Pair Your Device with Bluetooth or Speaker

Bluetooth headphones or speakers are required to listen to most audio on your Apple Watch (Siri, phone calls, voicemail, and voice memos play through the speaker on Apple Watch). Follow the headphones or speakers' instructions to put them in exploration mode. When your Bluetooth device is ready, proceed as follows:

1. Open the Apple Watch's Settings app, then tap Bluetooth.

2. When the device appears, tap it.

3. To open the Bluetooth setting, tap the AirPlay button on the play screens of the Audiobooks, Music, Now Playing, and Podcasts applications.

Adjust the Volume of Your Watch

1. Enter the Settings applications on your watch.

2. Touch the Sounds and Haptics button.

3. Touch the volume control in the Alert Volume section, click the slider, and rotate the Digital Crown.

Adjust the Haptic Intensity

You can change the intensity of the haptics—or wrist taps—the Apple Watch makes use of for alerts & notifications.

How to Receive and Send Payment through Apple Pay on Your Apple Watch

You can easily make payment on your Apple Watch through your personal Apple Pay in the Message App.

How to Make a Call Right from Your Wrist

You can use Siri to make a quick call. When Apple Watch is connected to a Wi-Fi or cellular connection, raise your wrist and say, "Call Dad."

How to Turn On/Off VoiceOver

1. Open the Settings app on your Apple Watch.

2. VoiceOver can be enabled by going to Accessibility > VoiceOver.

3. To turn off VoiceOver, double-tap the button.

4. Siri says, "Turn VoiceOver on" or "Turn VoiceOver off."

Check Your Apple Watch Storage

Storage on your Apple Watch displays what is taking up storage space. It displays the total amount used, the remaining amount, and how much storage space each app consumes.

Get More Apps for your Apple Watch

On Apple Watch, you can download new apps from the App Store. You can also use third-party apps that you already have on your iPhone to download new ones.

Using the Control Center

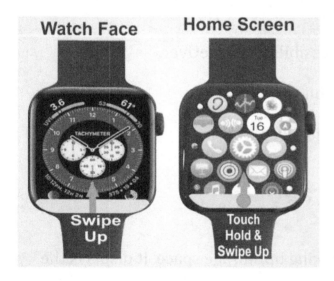

There are two major ways of opening the Control Center:

1. **Method of Observing Face Open** – This is the main Apple Watch face screen shows they watch. On this page, swipe up from the bottom of your Apple Watch screen with your finger.

2. **Method for Opening Apps' Home Screen** – To switch from the Watch Face to the Apps' Home Screen: Once, press the Digital Crown. Suppose you are already on the Apps Home screen. Swipe the screen with your finger from the bottom of the Apple Watch touch-hold (press and hold for 1 to 2 seconds). The Control Center will appear immediately.

In the Command and Control Center, you will see all of the aforementioned operational icons on the Control Center, which you can quickly use to meet your immediate need.

Step-by-Step Control Center Configuration

All of the following icons are available on your Apple Watch Series 7. However, the icon arrangement will differ from your Apple Watch Control Center because I have already rearranged all the icons to best meet my urgent needs.

Open the Control Center and scroll down the screen by turning the Digital Crown up or swiping up the screen with your finger to see more icons and the Edit button below.

How to Rearrange the Icons to Satisfy your Immediate Need

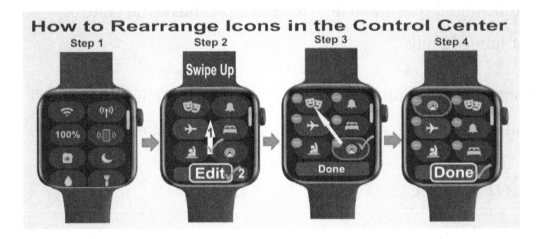

1. Tap the Edit button to make all of the icons movable.

2. A minus sign will appear at the top left of each icon, and the icons will shake.

3. Place your finger on the icon you want to move and drag it to the new location.

4. When you're finished rearranging the icons, click the Done button to the right to make your changes permanent.

How to Remove an Icon Button from the Control Center

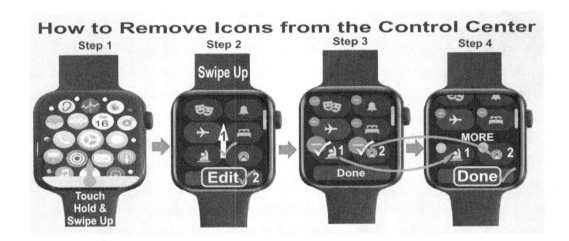

1. To open the Control Center, tap and hold the bottom of the App's Homescreen.

2. Scroll down and press the Edit button.

3. At the top left of each icon, you will see minus sign ⊖ and the icons will shake, then tap the Minus *sign.*

4. Immediate More will appear, and the removed Icon will show under the *Add* sign ⊕ at the top left of the Icon.

5. When you're finished, click the Done button to the right.

Chapter 6: How to Use Siri

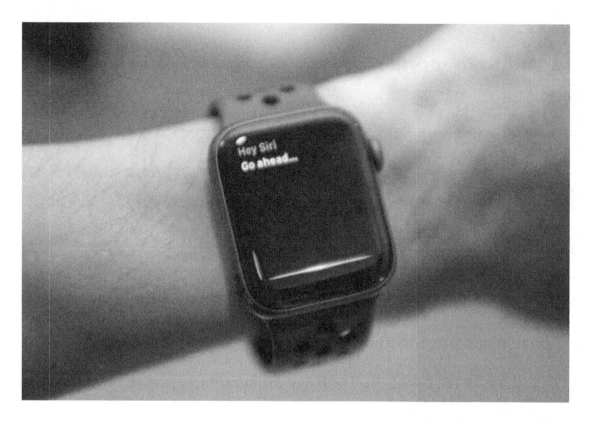

You can use Siri to perform tasks and receive responses on your Apple Watch. For example, after asking a broad question, Siri can translate your words into another language, recognize music and provide an instant Shazam answer, or display the top few search results along with a small excerpt from each page. To access the page, simply press the Open Page button on your Apple Watch.

When using Siri, you can say something like the following:

- "How do you say, 'How are you?' in Chinese?"

- "Begin a thirty-minute outdoor run."

- "Please notify Sandy that I am nearly finished."

- "Initialize the Sleep application."

- "Does this sound like a song?"

- "How do rainbows appear?"

- "How is it going for you?"

- "Can I ask you what kinds of questions?"

How to Make the Most of Siri

The Apple Watch must be connected to the internet to use Siri. There may be cellular service fees.

- Perform one of the following actions to start a Siri request:

  1. Raise your wrist and use your voice to communicate with your Apple Watch.

  2. To turn off Raise to Speak on your Apple Watch, open the Settings app, activate Siri, and then turn off Raise to Speak.

  3. Say "Hey Siri," followed by your request to summon Siri.

- To turn off "Hey Siri," open the Apple Watch Settings app, press Siri, and then toggle off. Listen out for "Hey Siri."

1. Tap the Siri button on the Siri watch face.

2. Hold down the Digital Crown until the listening indicator appears before your request.

- To disable the Press Digital Crown feature on your Apple Watch, navigate to the Settings app, activate Siri, and then disable Press Digital Crown. After you've activated Siri, you can relax your wrist. When there is a reaction, a tap will occur.

- Hold down the Digital Crown and speak to respond to a Siri query or to continue the conversation. Siri may respond verbally to you, as it does on iOS, iPad, and macOS. You can also use Bluetooth headphones or speakers connected to your Apple Watch to hear Siri's responses.

- To customize Siri's language and voice, open the Settings app on your Apple Watch, press Siri, and then select Language or Siri Voice. When you tap Siri Voice, you can customize the voice's variety and gender.

- You can use Siri to respond to a message quickly. If you have an Apple Watch with a Wi-Fi or cellular connection, raise your wrist, and say, "Tell Eve to meet me at 3." You can also respond with a Tapback by touching and holding the message and giving the sender a thumbs up.

- Modify the voice feedback settings. Siri on your Apple Watch can speak responses. Open the Settings app on your Apple Watch, then ask Siri to do one of the following: Siri is always available, even when your Apple Watch is in silent mode.

- Controlling in Silent Mode: When your Apple Watch is set to silent mode, Siri responses are muted.

- Siri only responds when your Apple Watch is connected to Bluetooth headphones.

Chapter 7: Apple Watch Default Apps and How to Find New Apps

Open Apps on Apple Watch

You can launch any app on your Apple Watch from the Home screen. The dock allows you to access the applications you use the most quickly. You can add up to ten applications to the dock to keep your favorite hands at your fingertips.

How to Change the Display of Your Apps to a Grid or List

The Home screen can display applications as a grid or list view. Follow these instructions to select one:

1. Touch the Home screen for a long time.

2. Select a grid view or list view.

How to Launch an Application

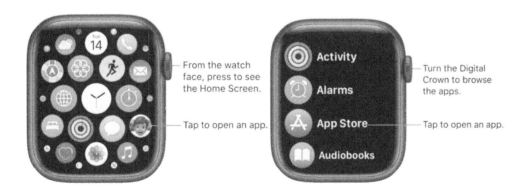

The format you select determines how to launch an application.

- **Grid Format:** Click on the grid format application icon. If you are already on your home screen, you can rotate the Digital Crown to launch the app in the center of your screen.

- **List View:** Rotate the Digital Crown and click on an application.

Press Crown Digital once to return to the home screen from an application and then again to access the watch face (or tap the clock icon on your Home Screen). Double-click the Digital Crown to quickly access the most recently used application while viewing another application or watch face.

How to Adjust Application Settings

1. Start the Watch app on your phone.

2. Click My Watch, then scroll down to see your installed apps.

3. To change the settings of an application, click on it.

4. View the storage that applications are using.

5. Navigate to the Settings app on your watch.

6. Navigate to General> Storage.

How to Launch the Application Store on Your Watch

1. To view the applications, rotate the Digital Crown.

2. To view more applications, select a category or tap See All under a collection.

3. To obtain a free application, click Get. To purchase the application, click on the price.

4. If you see a Download button instead of a price, you have already purchased the app and can download it for free. Some applications require an iOS version on your iPhone.

5. To find a specific application, click the Search box in the upper right corner of your screen, then type, or use Scribble or dictation, the application's name. You can also tap a category to see the most popular application categories.

Note: There may be mobile data charges when using the Apple Watch with cellular.

How to Organize Apps

1. Click on Digital Crown, Hold the Home Screen.

2. Hold an app and click on Edit to enable movement.

3. Move the app to any position you want.

4. Press Digital Crown when done.

How to Get More Apps for Your Watch

1. On your Apple Watch, open the App Store app.

2. Use the Digital Crown to navigate among highlighted applications.

3. To see other applications, choose a category or tap See All under a collection.

4. Tap Get to get a free app. To purchase an application, hit the pricing.

Chapter 8: Best Apps

Map App

How to get Directions

1. Open the Apple Watch Maps app.

2. Scroll through Favorites, Guides, and Recent by rotating the Digital Crown.

3. Touch the entry for driving, walking, public transportation, and biking directions. Please remember that not all modes of transportation are available at every location.

4. Touch the shape to see suggested routes, then tap the route to begin the journey and see an overview of the route, including turns, the distance between turns, and street names.

5. Look in the upper left corner for the estimated arrival time.

How to get Directions to the Point or Pin on the Map

1. Open the Apple Watch Maps app.

2. Touch Location, and then a destination or map marker.

3. Scroll through the location information until you reach Directions, then select walking, driving, public transportation, or cycling directions.

4. When you're ready, tap the route and follow the on-screen instructions.

How to View and Find Your Current Location and Surroundings

1. Open the Apple Watch Maps app.

2. Select Location.

3. Touch the more buttons, then Search Here to find your location.

4. Touch Public Transportation Map to view nearby public transportation options.

How to get Information About a Landmark or Marked Location

1. Touch the location marker on the map.

2. Rotate the Digital Crown to scroll through the information.

3. Touch < in the upper left corner to return to the map.

Weather App

Open the Weather app on your Watch to see the current temperature and weather conditions. Select a city and tap the display to get an hourly rain, weather, or temperature forecast.

How to Examine the Air Quality, UV Index, Wind Speed, and Ten-day Forecast

1. Tap a city to scroll down. Click in the upper left corner to return to the list of cities. Incorporate a city.

2. Navigate to your Watch's Weather app and press the button.

3. Select Add City from the dropdown menu at the bottom of the list of cities.

4. Enter the name of a city manually, sketch it down, or dictate it.

5. The Watch Series 7's Scribble feature is accessed by sliding up from the bottom of the screen and touching the word Scribble.

6. Select the city's name from the results list after clicking the Done button. The Weather app on the iPhone displays the same cities in the same order as the Weather app on the Apple Watch.

How to Remove the City

1. Navigate to your Watch's Weather app and press the button.

2. Swipe left on the city list until you reach the one you want to delete, then click the X icon.

3. The city will no longer be visible on your iPhone or Watch.

How to Select a Default City

1. It is accessible via the Settings menu. Select a city from the menu bar by clicking Weather, then Default City.

2. If you have an iPhone, open the Watch app, go to Weather>Default City, and select My Watch.

3. If you've added the weather to the watch face, you'll see the current weather conditions in your chosen city.

Message

In addition to reading and responding to text messages on your Apple Watch, you can do so by dictating an answer or switching to your iPhone and typing in an answer using a QWERTY keyboard, and QuickPath (available in English) Simplified Chinese exclusively on Apple Watch Series 7).

Read Messages on Apple Watch

1. After receiving a message and hearing a tap or buzzer, you can read it by raising your Apple Watch and looking down.

2. To confirm your selection, scroll down to the bottom of the message and select "Confirm."

3. To return to the message's introduction, swipe up from the bottom of the screen.

4. Tap and hold the top of the screen, then swipe down to reveal the notification if you've recently received one.

5. Scroll down and tap the Close button to mark the message as read. Press the Digital Crown button on your device's touchscreen to dismiss the notice without marking it as read.

Tip: You can access Apple Watch-optimized web content by clicking on the website link included in the notification. To magnify the material, double-tap the screen.

Determine the Date and Time the Message was Sent

In Messages, go to the Conversations menu and swipe left on a message within the conversation.

To Mute a Conversation

Swipe left and tap the Do Not Disturb icon to the left of a Messages conversation to mute it.

To Delete the Conversation

To access the Trash button, swipe left on any discussion in the Messages conversation list.

Music App

How to Add Music to Apple Watch

Using the Watch app on your iPhone, select tracks to sync with your Watch. When you transfer music to your Apple Watch, you can listen to it regardless of where your iPhone is. Using the Apple Watch app on your smartphone, you can sync playlists and albums to your Apple Watch and vice versa. If you own an Apple Watch and have an Apple Music subscription, you can also add music to it directly from the Music app on your iPhone or iPad.

It's worth noting that if you have an Apple Songs subscription, you won't be asked to choose music for your Apple Watch. A new track is automatically added to the playlist based on your most recently listened to music. Apple Songs will make recommendations if you haven't listened to music in a while.

1. Begin by opening the Watch app.

2. Select My Watch, then Music, and then OK.

3. From the Playlists and Albums dropdown menu, choose Add Music.

4. Select the albums and playlists from your computer that you want to sync with your Watch.

5. When you charge your Apple Watch and place it near your iPhone, music is automatically added to it.

How to Use Apple Watch to Add Music

If you have an active Apple Music subscription, you can use the Apple Watch to add music to an existing Apple Music playlist.

1. From the Start menu, select the Music program.

2. Select Library, Play Now or Search from the dropdown menu to find your music.

3. Click the More button after selecting a playlist or album from the dropdown menu.

4. A message confirms the addition of the item to the list.

5. To download music to your Watch, press the More symbol again, then the Download button.

6. Music is automatically added to the device when the Watch is turned on and connected to Wi-Fi.

How to Remove All Music from Your Apple Watch

It makes no difference whether the music was automatically or manually uploaded; if you have an Apple Music subscription, you can immediately remove it from your Watch.

1. To open the Music app, press the Music button on your Watch.

2. Go to the Library menu, Downloaded, and Playlists or Albums to view the contents of playlists and albums.

3. Swiping left on a playlist or album brings up the More menu, where you can select Delete.

4. Select Remove Download or Remove from Library from the menu.

It will be removed from your Watch, but it will remain in your music library, making it easier to find later. Remove from Library removes the item from your Apple Watch and any other Apple ID-enabled devices you own.

How to Use Your Apple Watch to Listen to Music

Music can be selected and played directly from the Apple Watch's Music app. You can use your Watch to listen to music, manage your iPhone, and stream music from Apple Music if you have a subscription.

The Music app will launch when you connect your Watch to Bluetooth headphones or speakers.

The album title appears in the upper left corner of the screen. The song title and artist are displayed in the top-left corner, the playback controls are in the center, and the AirPlay buttons, track list, and radio buttons are located in the bottom-right corner, among other things. To see album art, rotate the Digital Crown, tap a playlist or album to start and listen to it.

Blood Oxygen

1. On the Apple Watch, look for the Settings app.

2. Turn on Blood Oxygen Measurements after touching Blood Oxygen.

How to Disable Background Measurements in Sleep and Theater Modes

1. On the Apple Watch, look for the Settings app.

2. Touch Blood Oxygen, then turn off in sleep and theater modes.

Methods for Determining the Level of Oxygen in the Blood

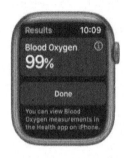

1. Navigate to the Apple Watch's Blood Oxygen app.

2. Place your hand on a table or your lap, with your wrist straight and the Apple Watch screen facing up.

3. Hold your hand still for a 15-second countdown after tapping Start. You will be notified of the results after the measurement. Done should be selected.

Contacts

The Contacts application allows you to browse, update, and exchange contacts from other Apple ID-enabled devices. You also have the option of creating contacts and personalizing contact cards.

The contact appears in the Contacts program. The contact's name and photo are displayed in the upper left and upper right corners, respectively.

How to Use the Contacts App

1. To contact someone, open the Contacts app on your Apple Watch and enter their information.

2. Rotate the Digital Crown to see a list of your contacts. When you tap a contact's name, you'll see their address and notes.

3. Enlarge an image associated with a contact by tapping it.

How to Keep in Touch with your Contacts

● To view the contact's phone numbers, click the Phone icon. Simply press the phone number to make a call.

● Click the Message button to open an existing message thread or start a new one.

● To begin composing an email message, click the Email button.

● To invite someone to the Walkie-Talkie or start a Walkie-Talkie chat, either click the Walkie-Talkie button or, if they have already accepted your invitation and have Walkie-Talkie enabled, click the Walkie-Talkie button.

Directly from the Contacts app, you can call, text, email, or hold a walkie-talkie conversation.

1. To contact someone, open your Apple Watch's Contacts app and enter their information.

2. You can scroll through your phone's contact list using the Digital Crown.

3. After tapping a contact, do one of the following:

How to Contact Someone

1. To contact someone, open the Contacts app on your Apple Watch and enter their information.

2. Select New Contact from the dropdown menu at the top of the screen.

3. Include the contact's name and, if applicable, the company.

4. Fill out the form with your phone number, email address, and mailing address, then click Done.

How to Share, Update, or Remove Contacts

1. To contact someone, open the Contacts app on your Apple Watch and enter their information.

2. Rotate the Digital Crown to see a list of your contacts.

3. Select a contact from the list and scroll down to the Share Contact, Edit Contact, or Delete Contact choices.

Camera

Choose option

Take a photo.

Your Watch can be used to view and manage the camera on your device remotely. You can also use the Watch to set the shutter timer, so you have enough time to lower your wrist and look up while still in the frame.

To use your Watch as a remote control, it must be within the Bluetooth range of your iPhone (about 33 feet or 10 meters).

The Watch is a remote control displaying what the camera sees on the iPhone's screen. The Take Snapshot button is in the lower right corner of the screen, and the More Options option is on the right side. If you've taken a photo, the photo view button is located in the screen's bottom-left corner.

To launch the Camera Remote application, do the following:

1. Press the button on the side. Simply move the Digital Crown to the desired location on the touchscreen to zoom in or out.

2. To change the exposure, drag the mouse over a large portion of the photo in the Watch preview.

All that is required to take a photograph is to press the shutter button on your camera.

This photograph has been saved to your iPhone's Photos app, but it can also be viewed on your Watch via the Watch app.

How to View Your Pictures

To view your images on your Watch, follow the steps below:

1. Select the thumbnail that appears in the lower-left corner of the screen.

2. Swipe left or right to see more photos.

3. Zoom in and out by rotating the digital crown.

4. To create a panoramic view, drag the magnified image around the screen.

5. You can finish the screen by double-tapping on the image.

6. You can change the position of the Close button and the number of photos displayed or hidden. To use it, simply tap the screen once.

7. When you've finished your work, click Close.

How to Alter the Settings on Another Camera

1. Start the Camera Remote app. You can select one of the following options by clicking the More Options button:

   a. Timing gadget (3-second timer on or off)

   b. Camcorder (front or rear)

c. Blitz (automatic, on, or off)

d. Real-time (automatic, on or off)

Mail

On Apple Watch, you can read your e-mail and respond with a QWERTY keyboard, QuickPath (exclusive to Apple Watch Series 7), dictation, drawing, emoji, or a pre-written message. You can also use your iPhone's Watch app, which is available for iOS devices.

1. Examine the email notification.

2. When you receive a new notification, simply raise your wrist to read it.

3. Scroll down the watch screen to reveal the unread alerts and tap the missed notification if you miss a notification.

If you accidentally miss a notification, simply slide down the watch display to reveal unread alerts and tap the notification that appears.

To customize your Watch's email notifications, launch the Watch app and go to My Watch> Mail> Personalize.

How to Use the Mail App to Read Email

1. Launch the Mail application.

2. Turn the Digital Crown clockwise to cycle through the list of messages.

3. Simply tap on a message to read it. The Digital Crown or the top of the screen can be turned to advance to the beginning of a lengthy message.

The Mail program displayed an email message. The recipient's name appears first, followed by the subject line and message body.

Messages on the Apple Watch have been optimized for viewing. While most text styles have been preserved, Apple Watch-optimized site content is available by clicking on webpage links in Mail. To enlarge the material, double-tap it.

How to Reply to a Message

Scroll down to respond to a message from the Mail app. If the message is intended for a group of people, select Reply All from the dropdown menu. Choose Add Message from the dropdown menu.

As you scroll down the page, you will see a list of frequently used phrases; select one, and the phrase will be sent to you.

Then go to Messages > Canned Replies > Add Reply and type your statement into the box. To rearrange the prepared responses, click Edit and drag them around the screen. Alternatively, you can use the Erase option to remove the answer from the system completely.

Smart Answers can be translated into another language by scrolling down to Languages and selecting a language from the dropdown box that appears. The languages available on your iPhone have been enabled in Settings> General> Keyboard> Keyboards on your iOS device.

After clicking the button, enter your response in the "Add message" section.

You Can Check Your Email on an iPhone

Wake your iPhone and open the app switcher to respond to an incoming call on your preferred mobile device. To pause a video on an iPhone with Face ID, swipe up from the bottom edge of the screen.

You can open an email in the Mail application by clicking the button at the bottom of the screen.

Chapter 9: Very Detailed Health and Fitness About All Functions

Apple Fitness

Begin Your Workout

1. On your Apple Watch, launch the Workout app.

2. Adjust the Digital Crown to the desired workout.

3. At the bottom of the screen, tap Add Workout to add activities such as kickboxing or surfing.

4. Tap the More icon to add a goal.

5. Choose a calorie, time, distance, or open goal (if you don't have a specific goal in mind but want your Apple Watch to log your workout).

6. To set, turn the Digital Crown or tap + / –.

7. Tap Start when you're ready to begin.

As you interact with the app and select workouts, the order of the workouts is determined by your preferences.

To begin a workout without a goal, choose the type of workout you want—a run, stroll, or stair stepper.

Determine an appropriate pace for an outdoor run session. Select the desired pace for an outdoor run, and your Apple Watch will tap you on the wrist after one mile to inform you whether you're ahead or behind schedule.

1. On your Apple Watch, launch the Workout app.

2. Scroll to Outdoor Run using the Digital Crown, then hit the More button.

3. Tap Set Alert, followed by OK.

4. Adjust the desired time for running a mile—for example, 9 minutes—and tap Done.

5. Tap to select Average or Rolling. Average is your average pace throughout all miles run, while Rolling is the pace at which you are traveling one mile.

Throughout your workouts, your Apple Watch recalls your intended pace. To alter it, select Outdoor Run, hit the More icon, and tap the currently selected pace. Combining various activities into a single workout is a great way to maximize your results.

How to End and Review Your Workout

Workouts are completed using Apple Watches. You will hear a tone and feel a vibration when you achieve your goal. If you're feeling good and want to keep going, you can—your Apple Watch will continue to collect data until you tell it to stop. When you're ready to call it a day, do the following: Swipe right, then press End.

Scroll through the results summary using the Digital Crown, then click Done at the bottom. After you finish a workout, the heart rate sensor will remain active for three minutes to monitor your heart rate recovery. After finishing a workout, tap the heart icon to see your progress in real-time.

Consider Your Previous Workouts

1. Launch the Fitness app on your iPhone.

2. Choose Summary, then a workout.

3. To view a specific type of workout, such as Walking or Swimming, tap Show More next to Workouts, then tap All Workouts.

4. Tap the name of the workout in the top-right corner, then tap All Workouts in the resulting list to return to the list of all workouts.

To consider your route and pace during your workout: Open the Fitness app on your iPhone. Choose Summary, then an exercise. Finally, beneath the Map, click on the map thumbnail. The route offers opportunities for walking, hiking, running, open water swimming, and cycling. Your speed is represented by the colors on your route, with green being the fastest and red being the slowest. You must enable route tracking to see the route. Route tracking can be enabled during or after the initial setup of your Apple Watch:

In the Apple Watch app, go to In the Settings app, to Privacy > Locations Services, tap Apple Watch Workout, and then tap While Using the App.

Use Apple Watch to Check Your Heart Rate

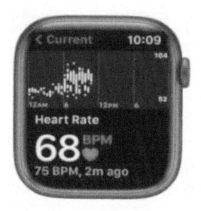

Your heart rate is a crucial indicator of how well your body functions. You can track your heart rate while exercising and your resting, walking, breathing, workout, and recovery rates throughout the day, and take a new reading at any time.

To view your current heart rate, resting rate, and walking average rate, open the Heart Rate app on your Apple Watch. Your Apple Watch will monitor your heart rate as long as you wear it.

How to Set Up Your Health Card

1. On your iPhone, activate the Health app.

2. Tap your profile picture in the upper right corner, then tap Doctor ID.

3. Tap Get Started and fill in your information.

Steps to View Your Healthcare ID on Apple Watch

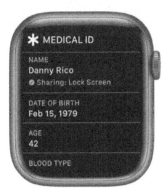

1. Press and hold the side button on your Apple Watch until the sliders appear.

2. Drag the Clinician ID slider to the right.

If your health card isn't visible when you press and hold the side button on your Apple Watch, open the Apple Watch app on your iPhone, touch My Watch, tap Health, click Health Card, then hit Edit "And turn on" Show When Obscured." Turn off Show When Locked to hide your medical record when your Apple Watch is locked.

If you add emergency contacts to your medical ID, your Apple Watch will notify them if you make an SOS call to an ambulance.

Set Up Hand Washing on Apple Watch

Your Apple Watch can detect when you begin washing and encourage you to wash for 20 seconds, as recommended by global health organizations. Your Apple Watch will notify you if you haven't cleaned your hands within minutes of returning home. Here is how to make handwashing possible:

1. Activate the Settings app on your Apple Watch.

2. Turn on the Hand Wash timer after touching Hand Wash.

3. When Apple Watch detects that you are washing your hands, it sets a timer for 20 seconds. If you stop washing in less than 20 seconds, be sure to stop working.

Managing Your Sleep on Your Watch

1. Follow the instructions on your display. You can also open the Health app on your phone, select Browse and Sleep, and then select Get Started in the Setup Sleep section.

Change or Disable Your Next Wake-Up Alarm

1. Launch the Sleep application on your watch.

2. Tap on the current bedtime.

3. Touch wakeup time, rotate the Digital Crown to select a new wakeup time, and click the Check button to create a new wakeup time.

4. Deactivate the Alarm if you do not want your watch to wake you up in the morning. This modification only applies to your next wake-up alarm, after which your routine will resume.

5. Change or add sleep schedules. On your watch, launch the Sleep app.

6. Touch Full Schedule, then one of the following:

   a) **Schedule a change:** Select the current one by clicking on it.

   b) **Include a sleep schedule:** Select Add Schedule.

   c) **Change your sleep goal:** Touch your Sleep Goal, then select the amount of time you want to sleep.

   d) **Alter the wind-down time:** Touch Wind Down, then select how long you want sleep mode to be active before bed.

   e) **Alter the wake and sleep times:** Touch Wakeup or Bedtime, then rotate the Digital Crown to set a new time.

   f) **Set the alarm options:** Deactivate or activate Alarm on or off and select an alarm sound by pressing Sound.

How to delete or cancel a sleep schedule: To delete a schedule, click the Delete Schedule button at the bottom of your screen or the Cancel button (at the top of your screen) to stop creating a new one.

Track Your Menstrual Cycle

Cycle tracking is a tool that allows you to monitor and make informed decisions about the complexities of your menstrual cycle. It is possible to provide information on symptoms such as headaches or seizures and flow rate information. The Cycle Tracking app can notify you when your next period or fertility period will likely begin based on your recorded data. The app may also use Apple Watch heart rate data to improve prediction accuracy. Here is how to establish a cycle track:

1. Fire up the Cycle Tracking app.

2. Enter your GPS coordinates here. You can select parameters that affect the cycle by clicking on the control panel buttons, such as the flow rate and symptoms.

3. The observations are saved in the iPhone's cycle log and can be viewed later. If you enable menstruation and fertility prediction in your device's Health app, the Watch will send notifications about upcoming periods and fertility windows.

Chapter 10: The Apple Watch Series 8

The Apple Watch Series 8 is the latest iteration of Apple's popular smartwatch. Launched in 2022, the Series 8 features a range of new and improved features, including updates to its design, wellness capabilities, and connectivity. In this chapter, we will take a closer look at Series 8 and explore its key features and benefits.

Design and Display

Series 8 has undergone significant changes in design and materials. It features a more refined, polished, and modern design with a sleek, seamless case that integrates with a new always-on OLED display. The new display features improved brightness, contrast, and color accuracy, making it more legible and easier to read in all lighting conditions.

The Series 8 is also available in new colors, including graphite, gold, silver, and blue. The Series 8 has a slightly larger display than the Series 7, measuring 44mm or 40mm compared to 41mm or 45mm for the Series 7. The Series 8's display also features a new technology called MicroLED, which offers better brightness, color accuracy, and power efficiency than the Series 7's display.

In terms of design, the Series 8 has a more refined and premium look, with a flat-edged design similar to the latest iPhone models. The Series 7, on the other hand, has a more rounded design and a smaller bezel. Additionally, the watch's new ceramic shield front cover provides enhanced durability and drop protection.

Wellness Features

The Series 8 includes several new health and fitness features, including advanced sleep tracking capabilities, which help users monitor and improve their sleep quality. It also includes improved blood oxygen monitoring, which provides more accurate and detailed data on oxygen levels in the blood, and an updated ECG sensor, which can detect irregular heart rhythms.

The Series 8 offers several new wellness features, including a redesigned Mindfulness app and a new Respiratory Rate measurement. The Series 7 also has a Mindfulness app, but it doesn't have the Respiratory Rate feature.

Both watches offer blood oxygen monitoring, ECG, and fall detection, but the Series 8 has an additional feature called Tai Chi, which tracks your movements during this low-impact exercise.

Connectivity and Compatibility

The Series 8 includes improved cellular and Wi-Fi connectivity, which makes it easier for users to stay connected on the go, but it offers faster charging speeds thanks to a new USB-C charging cable. The watch supports 5G and LTE connectivity, providing faster data speeds and greater network coverage. It also includes Wi-Fi 6, which delivers faster and more reliable wireless connectivity.

The Series 8 is also compatible with the latest Apple devices and operating systems, while the Series 7 may not be able to run the latest software updates. It also integrates with third-party apps and services, allowing users to access a wide range of apps and functions directly from their watch.

Battery Life and Charging

The Series 8 features improved battery life and charging speeds, which means users can spend more time using their watch and less time charging it. The watch includes a new charging system that provides faster and more efficient charging, with a full charge taking only 45 minutes. Both the Series 7 and the Series 8 have all-day battery life, but the Series 8's battery is slightly larger, offering up to 18 hours of use on a single charge compared to 15 hours for the Series 7.

To optimize battery usage on the Series 8, users can enable low power mode and adjust their watch's settings, such as brightness and haptic feedback. The watch also includes a power reserve mode, allowing users to continue using basic functions even when the battery is low.

Price and Availability

The Series 8 is available in a range of models and configurations, with prices starting at $399. The watch is available for purchase directly from Apple and select retailers, with availability varying by region. Users can choose from various straps and bands to customize their watch's appearance and functionality.

Choosing the right Series 8 watch for your needs depends on your intended usage and preferences. For example, users who plan to use the watch primarily for fitness tracking may want to opt for a model with advanced health metrics, while those who need to stay connected on the go may prefer a cellular model.

Final Thoughts

The Apple Watch Series 8 is a powerful and versatile smartwatch that offers a range of new and improved features, including updates to its design, wellness capabilities, connectivity, and battery life. Whether you're a fitness enthusiast, a busy professional, or simply looking for a reliable and stylish watch, the Series 8 offers something for everyone.

To get the most out of your Series 8 watch, it's important to explore its features and settings and experiment with different apps and services. Whether you're using the watch for fitness tracking, mobile payments, messaging, or entertainment, there are endless possibilities for customization and personalization.

One of the biggest advantages of the Series 8 is its compatibility with a wide range of other Apple devices and services, such as the iPhone, iPad, and AirPods. This makes it easy to stay connected and productive throughout your day, whether you're at home, at work, or on the go.

Regarding pricing and availability, the Series 8 is positioned at the top of the Apple Watch lineup, with a range of different models and configurations to choose from. While the higher price point may be a consideration for some users, the added features and performance of the Series 8 make it a worthwhile investment for many.

Chapter 11: Best Tips and Tricks

Turn On the Always-On Display

The Apple Watch Series 5 was the first device to include Apple's new Always-on Display. You can now see everything at a glance without having to worry about your battery dying throughout the day. Furthermore, the Always-on Display on the Apple Watch Series 7 is nearly 70% brighter than the previous generation, making it easier to see in bright conditions. If the AOD function isn't enabled by default, here's how to enable it on the Apple Watch Series 7 device:

1. Select General from the Apple Watch's Settings app.

2. Select Display & Brightness from the menu bar to change the display and brightness.

3. Look for the "Always On" switch that can be found at the bottom of the page. The Always On toggle switch has now been set to "On."

Noise Notifications

Did you know that the music you listen to could damage your hearing? It's a problem we've all encountered at some point in our lives, as blasting our favorite music at maximum volume results in hearing loss. A similar issue arises if you spend an extended period in a noisy environment, such as a concert or construction site. "Noise Notifications" have been added by Apple to indicate when the volume is too high, when it should be turned down (if possible), or when earplugs should be used.

1. Start the Watch app on your iPhone.

2. Choose the My Watch tab at the bottom of the app.

3. Choose Noise.

4. Tap Noise Threshold.

5. Select one of the following: Off, a volume of 80%, 85 dB, 90 dB, or 95 dB equals one hundred decibels.

Sleep Tracking

1. Open the Settings app on your Watch.

2. Scroll to the bottom of the page and click the Sleep button.

3. To enable Sleep Tracking and Charging Reminders, follow the on-screen instructions.

Once you've agreed, you'll be awakened the following day by either a silent haptic alarm or gentle sounds. The Watch will summarize your day, including how much battery life you have left and how well you slept.

People who habitually do not charge their watches sufficiently to keep them running through the night will also be notified if their battery is running low. A notification will appear to remind you to charge your watch before going to bed.

Enable Screenshots

Screenshots are one of those "features" that have become second nature recently, from the Notes app to sharing memes with friends. While we don't use our Apple Watches as frequently as we do our iPhones, there may be times when a screenshot is required. Surprisingly, this feature is not enabled by default, but it is simple to enable.

Launch the Watch Application on your iPhone.

1. Select My Watch from the toolbar at the bottom of the screen.

2. Select General from the dropdown menu.

3. Toggle Enable Screenshots from the dropdown menu at the bottom of the page.

Portraits Watch Face

Apple revealed that the Photos watch face is the most popular date option during the watchOS eight introductions. WatchOS 8 includes the Portraits watch face, which has a dynamic, multi-layered appearance, to capitalize on the trend. Also included is information on how to use it with the Apple Watch Series 7.

1. Launch the Watch app on your iPhone.

2. The toolbar at the bottom of the screen provides access to the Face Gallery. The Portraits section can be found by scrolling to the left under "New Watch Faces."

3. Select Photos from the Content menu.

4. Choose a photo from your library to serve as the watch face. Select the Style dropdown menu from the clock style you want to use.

5. Select the Top and Bottom complications to investigate under Complications.

6. In the upper right corner, tap the Add button beneath the name.

This means that whatever image you choose will be more visible than ever before, which is ideal if you want to be cheered up every time you lift your wrist to check your watch.

Making Use of the QWERTY Keyboard

Because of the larger display, the Watch now has a full-sized QWERTY keyboard. This can be tapped (as usual) or moved around with QuickPath. QuickPath, according to Apple, will use on-device machine learning to predict the next word as you type.

Furthermore, Apple's apps now have larger buttons thanks to watchOS 8 on the Series 7.

Using the QWERTY keyboard, you can enter characters sequentially or move your finger from one letter to the next (American English and Simplified Chinese only; Apple Watch Series 7 only). To finish a word, remove your finger from the keyboard. Slide up from the bottom of the screen and click on the Keyboard button to access the keyboard.

Customize Notifications

The Apple Watch is ideal for people who want to track their activity and receive notifications daily. It's easy to become distracted with so many apps buzzing and blaring at you. Certain apps allow you to "customize notifications," giving you more say over what buzzes your wrist next.

1. Launch the Watch app on your iPhone.

2. At the bottom of the page, click the My Watch tab.

3. Select Notifications from the dropdown menu.

4. Select the app you want to change the alerts and click "Save."

5. If you want to mirror alerts between your iPhone and your Watch, select Mirror my iPhone from the dropdown menu.

Certain applications will display the following options:

- **Accept Notifications:** Notifications are displayed in the Notification Center, and notifications are sent to your Watch. Notifications are delivered to the Notification Center directly, bypassing your Watch.

- **Disabled Notifications:** The app does not send any notifications.

In rare cases, you cannot change the notification settings on your Apple Watch. Instead, you'll be limited to the app's "default" settings, or you can use the Mirror my iPhone feature.

Personalize Message Reactions

While canned responses can be useful in an emergency, they are not always the best option. You can, however, customize the "canned" custom responses you send when you receive a message.

1. On your iPhone, launch the Watch app.

2. The My Watch tab is located near the bottom of the app.

3. Scroll to the bottom of the page and select Messages.

4. From the dropdown menu, select Default Replies.

5. Choose one of the messages to be replaced.

6. To begin, type your personalized response.

Unlocking Your Mac

For Apple Watch owners who own Macs, the ability to use your Apple Watch to unlock your Mac (auto-unlock) and, for those running macOS Catalina and higher, to unlock your apps without entering a passcode is a useful feature. Simply double-tap the Apple Watch's Side button to validate passwords or authorize program installations on your Mac.

However, for this to work, you must first enable the feature. You must use the same Apple ID on both your Mac and Apple Watch:

1. On your Mac, go to System Preferences.

2. From the drop-down menu, select Security & Privacy.

3. Check the box next to Under General, and you can use your Apple Watch to unlock apps and your Mac.

After you've configured everything, you'll be able to wake your Mac and authorize app requests easily. Walk (or sit) close to your Mac and press any keyboard key to wake it up. Open the display cover if you have a MacBook or a MacBook Pro.

When the app requests permission, you will have no interaction with your Mac. Instead, the Apple Watch will vibrate to alert you, followed by a message instructing you to Double-Click to Approve. When you double-click the Side Button, your Mac will grant the request immediately.

Chapter 12: Maintenance

Use a soft, lint-free cloth to clean your Apple Watch. If necessary, lightly dampen the cloth with fresh water. Alternatively, you can immerse your Apple Watch for 10 to 15 seconds in lightly running, warm, fresh water. Soaps and other cleaning products are strictly prohibited.

All Apple Watch bands will become dirty over time. Dust, food, sweat, lotions, and other substances can all affect the appearance of your watch band. Your specific situation determines the frequency with which an Apple Watch band should be cleaned. Cleaning should be done as needed, but at least every two weeks.

To clean your Apple Watch properly, you will need the following items: a lint-free, soft, damp cloth. Isopropyl alcohol with at least 70% alcohol content and a clean cloth or similar disinfecting wipes

Cleaning and disinfecting your Apple Watch is similar to cleaning and disinfecting your iPhone or other "high-touch" device. Apple revised its cleaning instructions in response to the early 2020 coronavirus outbreak to encourage the use of isopropyl alcohol to kill bacteria, viruses, and other harmful microbes.

A toothpick or soft toothbrush is commonly used to loosen stuck-on dirt and grime from your watch. You can also use the following items to clean your Apple Watch properly:

- A lint-free, soft, damp cloth
- Isopropyl alcohol with a minimum alcohol content of 70% and a clean cloth or similar disinfecting wipes
- Cotton swabs (Q-Tips)
- A sink with hot and cold running water
- Soft-bristled toothbrush (optional)
- Toothpick made of wood (optional)

By removing the band, you can easily clean your Apple Watch. Remove your watch and turn it, so the back is facing you. The top and bottom of the rear sensor have two depressible buttons.

All Apple Watch bands will become dirty over time. Dust, food, sweat, lotions, and other substances can all affect the appearance of your watch band. Your specific situation determines the frequency with which an Apple Watch band should be cleaned. Cleaning should be done as needed, but at least every two weeks.

A lightly dampened cloth can be used to clean most Apple Watch bands. The amount of water and/or soap that can be used is heavily influenced by the watch band's material:

- **Silicone:** Silicone Apple Watch bands can be cleaned with warm water and hand soap because they are water resistant. Harsh cleaning agents should be avoided because they may degrade the protective coating that wraps around the band.

- **Leather:** Leather is not waterproof, contrary to popular belief. As a result of absorbing water, leather will deform or lose its color. When wet leather dries, it will almost certainly crack. As a result, leather bands should never be immersed in water (not even running water). If it gets wet, it should be wiped immediately (for example, from rain). Wiping down leather with a dry cloth or, if necessary, a lightly moistened cloth is recommended (and then drying immediately).

- **Nylon**: Apple Watch bands made entirely of nylon should be cleanable with a damp cloth. Remember that nylon absorbs moisture and must be thoroughly dried (otherwise, it will start to smell if the water stays inside the material). As a result, while it can be cleaned under running water or even in a washing machine, we do not recommend it unless all other options have been exhausted.

- **Stainless Steel:** Stainless steel is a type of metal. Apple Watch bands of 316L stainless steel can be cleaned with warm water and hand soap. Avoid harsh cleaning agents because they can degrade and change the color of the protective coating around the band. When using a lot of water (for example, washing it under running water), be careful because the design of those bands frequently traps water in crevices.

- **Wood:** Wooden Apple Watch bands, like leather bands, should not be washed. Because varnished wood is more water resistant, wipe it down with a lightly moistened cloth (and then dry immediately). Water exposure causes wood deformation and/or cracking in most cases.

What About the Straps and the Adapter?

They are made of stainless steel and can be cleaned with a damp cloth or even running water (if the material allows).

What about Hybrid Bands?

Hybrid Bands are bands made of two materials. When cleaning hybrid plants, you must clean them as if they were the most delicate material to avoid damaging them. Consider a nylon and leather Apple Watch band. Clean the band as you would a leather band because leather is more delicate.

After cleaning your Apple Watch band, we recommend that you thoroughly dry it. If you don't use much water, you won't have to spend much time drying. If you washed it with running water, take special care to get water out of crevices and other hard-to-reach areas. We recommend using a paper towel to absorb any water or moisture. You can use a hair dryer if you suspect that water has become trapped in an area that a paper towel cannot reach (with zero heat. Just blow out room-temperature air).

How to Alter the Position of Your Hands or Digital Crown

If you want to wear the Apple Watch on the other wrist or pull the Digital Crown in the opposite direction, adjust the orientation settings so that lifting your wrist awakens the Apple Watch, and sliding the Digital Crown moves everything in the appropriate direction.

1. Launch the Settings app on your Apple Watch.

2. From the General menu, choose Orientation.

3. Launch the Apple Watch app on your iPhone, tap My Watch, and then go to General > Watch Alignment.

How to Take Off and Replace Bands

1. Tape the Apple Watch to release it.

2. Slide the ribbon out, then slide the replacement ribbon in.

3. To insert a tape into the slot, never use force. If removing or inserting a tape is difficult, repeatedly press the tape release button.

How to Change the Apple Watch Band

1. The first step is to ensure you use the correct band size for your Apple Watch.

2. Place your watch's face on a clean surface, such as a microfiber cloth or a soft padded mat.

3. If you have a Link Bracelet, you can separate the band by pressing the Release button on a link. Long-press the band's release button, then slide the band away from your watch.

4. If the band does not slide out, press the release button once more and ensure you hold down the button while removing the band.

5. Ensure the band text is facing you and slide the new band till you hear & feel a click.

Solo Loop

If you own a Braided Solo Loop or Solo Loop, just drag from the band's bottom to extend the band over your wrist when putting it on and taking it off.

Milanese Loop

You can fully open the Milanese Loop band by sliding the magnetic block through the lug or band connector.

How to Remove the Link Bracelet

Before removing the band from your Watch, you must divide the Link Bracelet into two parts. Do not twist or force the band when removing it. To avoid damaging the clasp or band, follow the instructions below:

1. Close the butterfly's closure.

2. If the closure is open, fold it one side at a time until you hear a click.

3. Long-Press the quick release key. The release keys are inside the bracelet. You just have to long-press one of the buttons.

4. Remove the links gently. Long-press the release key while pulling. Separate the band into two pieces before you remove the band from your watch.

5. Remove the band. Press your band's release button and slide your watch band to remove it.

Restart, Reset, Restore, and Update

If something isn't working properly, try restarting your watch and the phone with which it's paired.

To turn your watch off, long-press the side button until the sliders appear, then slide the Power Off slider to the right.

To turn on your watch, long-press the side button until the Apple logo appears on the screen.

Restart Your Watch

If you cannot turn off your watch or if the problem persists, you can force it to restart. Only do this if you can't restart your watch.

Long-press the side button and the Digital Crown simultaneously for about 10 seconds, or until the Apple icon appears on your display to force restart your watch.

You must note that you cannot restart a charging Apple Watch.

Erase Your watch

You may sometimes need to erase your watch, such as when you forget your password.

Navigate to the Settings app on your watch.

Go to General> Reset, select Erase All Content & Settings and enter your passcode.

If you can't access the Settings application on your watch because you forgot your password, plug it in and hold down the side button until Power Off appears on your screen. Touch the Reset button after long pressing the Digital Crown.

After the reset is complete and your watch restarts, you must reconnect the Apple Watch to the iPhone.

Use a Backup to Restore Your Watch

Your watch automatically backs up to your paired phone, and you can restore it from a saved backup.

Backup and Restore Your Watch

Back Up Your Watch

When paired with your phone, your watch is constantly backed up to your phone. When you unpair your watch from your phone, a backup is created. You can restore your watch from a backup by selecting Restore from Back Up and selecting a saved backup on your phone when pairing your watch with the same phone again or when pairing a new watch with that same iPhone.

Update the Software on Your Watch

Software updates should be checked for and installed.

1. Launch the Watch app on your iPhone.

2. Click My Watch, go to General> Software Updates, and then click Download & Install. If an update is available, click Download & Install.

Chapter 13: FAQ

What is Unique about Apple Watch and WatchOS 8?

The latest Apple Watch offers more screen real estate with smaller bezels and an edge-breaking effect, the largest and most advanced display, the longest-lasting Apple Watch, and fast charging (Apple Watch Series 7). The Apple Watch Series 7 charges faster than any previous model thanks to its integrated USB-C connector. Please keep in mind that not all locations offer quick charging.

WatchOS 8.1 Immunization or Vaccination Card: Save your immunization or vaccination record to your iPhone's Health app, your Apple Watch's Wallet app, or your iPad's Health app, and then double-click the side button to display it.

How to Discover New Watch Faces?

New watch faces for the Apple Watch include World Time, which displays the time in multiple time zones, portraits, Apple Watch Series 7, Contour, and dual modular.

How Do You Enjoy A Moment of Awareness in your Apple Watch?

The new Reflect function in the Mindfulness app assists you in developing a meditation practice by focusing on a brief and thought-provoking topic. With an Apple Fitness Plus subscription, you can listen to guided meditations on your Apple Watch.

How Do You Find Misplaced Devices and Objects?

You can find lost Apple and AirTag devices and friends with the new "Find Gadgets" and "Find Items" applications for Apple Watch.

How Do You Reconnect with Significant People, Places, and Events?

Photo highlights from your memories and popular images connect to your watch automatically and deliver something new every day.

How Do You Stay Focused?

Focus allows you to stay in the present moment and receive only the alerts you want. Select a predefined focus, such as work or fitness, or sync a custom focus from your iPhone, iPad, or Mac.

How Do You Use Your Apple Watch to Unlock Your Mac?

When your Mac wakes up from sleep, your Apple Watch can quickly unlock it. Before using this fantastic feature, both devices must be signed in to iCloud with the same Apple ID, Bluetooth, and Wi-Fi must be enabled on both devices, and your Mac model must be mid-2013 or later.

1. On your Mac, enable Auto Unlock.

2. Select the Apple menu > System Preferences on your Mac.

3. Click Security & Privacy > General, then select Allow your Apple Watch to unlock your Mac or Use your Apple Watch to unlock apps and your Mac.

How Do You Restart Your Device?

If something isn't working properly, try resetting both your Series 7 device and the iPhone with which it is paired.

1. Restart the Apple Watch.

2. Hold the side button until the sliders appear, then slide the Power Off slider to the right.

3. To turn on your Apple Watch, press the side button until you see the Apple logo.

It is important to note that your Apple Watch cannot be restarted while charging.

How Do You Restore Your Device?

Your Apple Watch is automatically backed up to your connected iPhone, from which you can restore it. Backups of your Apple Watch are included with backups of your iPhone, whether to iCloud or your Mac or PC. You cannot access your backups if they are stored in iCloud. Make a backup of your Apple Watch and restore it if necessary.

Create an Apple Watch backup: When your Series 7 device is connected to an iPhone, its data is automatically backed up to the iPhone. When you unplug the devices, a backup is first created.

Follow these steps to restore your Series 7 device from a backup: If you re-pair your Apple Watch with the same iPhone or purchase a new Apple Watch, you can select Restore from Backup and an iPhone backup.

1. Perform a software update check and install any necessary updates.

2. On your iPhone, open the Apple Watch app.

3. Navigate to My Watch.

4. Then select General > Software Update.

5. Finally, press the Download and Install button if an update is available.

How Do You Erase Your Device?

You may need to erase your Series 7 device in some cases, such as if you forget your passcode.

1. Delete your Apple Watch's settings and data.

2. On your Series 7 device, launch the Settings app.

3. Select General > Reset, followed by Erase All Content and Settings.

If you use your device with a cellular plan, you have two options: Erase All or Erase All & Keep Plan. Select Erase All to delete your Apple Watch entirely. Select Erase All & Keep Plan if you want to erase everything and restore it with your cellular plan intact.

Additionally, open the Apple Watch app on your iPhone, click My Watch, General > Reset, and finally, Erase Apple Watch Content and Settings.

If you cannot access the Settings app on your Series 7 device due to forgotten passcode, charge it and hold down the side button until Power Off appears. Tap Reset after pressing and holding the Digital Crown.

After you've reset and restarted your device, you'll need to repair it with your iPhone— open the Apple Watch app and follow the on-screen instructions.

How Do You Make Use of the Braille Display?

Use a braille display with VoiceOver on the Apple Watch: The Apple Watch is compatible with a wide range of international braille tables and reloadable braille displays. You can connect a Bluetooth wireless braille display to view VoiceOver output, such as contracted and uncontracted braille.

Conclusion

The Apple Watch 7 includes numerous new and improved features. You have learned about and mastered these cool Apple Watch features by diving into this book.

According to Apple's chief operating officer, Apple Watch Series 7 includes critical upgrades ranging from our largest and most advanced display to improved durability and faster charging, making the world's best smartwatch better than ever before. "Powered by watchOS 8, it brings valuable new capacities to help clients stay connected, track action and exercises, and better comprehend their overall wellbeing and health," said Apple's chief working official.

The Apple Watch Series 7 has a more durable screen, rounded edges, a better Retina display, faster charging, and a larger screen than its predecessor. A sensor in the smartwatch measures the user's health and fitness level. It has many features such as fall detection, blood oxygen monitoring, heart rate monitoring, workout tracking with voice feedback, loud noise detection, handwashing detection, sleep tracking, a mindfulness app, ECG readings, and many more. Apple has added Tai Chi and Pilates workouts and the ability to call 911 in an emergency.

The Apple Watch 7's larger screen also lets you see notifications at a glance and respond with the new QWERTY keyboard. It also has a brighter, always-on display, allowing you to see the time and certain complications on your watch without tapping the screen or raising your wrist. It has a faster chip, a better processor, a longer battery life, faster charging, and numerous other improvements.

The Apple Watch Series 7 has an Always redesigned On Retina screen with significantly more screen area and thinner lines than previous models, making it the largest and most developed screen of all time. The smaller boundaries allow the presentation to increase screen area while slightly altering the actual watch's components. The Apple Watch Series 7 has a refined design with milder, more adjusted corners. The presentation has an extraordinary refractive edge that consistently associates full-screen watch faces and applications with the case's bend. With the enhancements to the showcase, clients benefit from a similar all-day 18-hour battery life.

Because of a clever design that expands the screen region while barely changing the components of the overall case size, Apple Watch Series 7 is available in 41mm and 45mm sizes. The Apple Watch Series 7 features a redesigned front precious stone with a more grounded and vigorous calculation that is more than 50% thicker than the Apple Watch Series 6, making it more break safe without sacrificing optical clarity. The Apple Watch Series 7 is dust-proof (IP6X), making it more durable in environments such as the ocean or the desert while maintaining excellent swimming performance (WR50).

Thank you for taking the time to read this book. Good luck.